中华人民共和国文化和旅游部
2024年文化和旅游发展统计公报

STATISTICAL COMMUNIQUÉ OF THE MINISTRY OF CULTURE AND TOURISM OF THE PEOPLE'S REPUBLIC OF CHINA ON CULTURAL AND TOURISM DEVELOPMENT IN 2024

中华人民共和国文化和旅游部 编

中国统计出版社
China Statistics Press

图书在版编目（CIP）数据

中华人民共和国文化和旅游部2024年文化和旅游发展统计公报 = Statistical Communique of the Ministry of Culture and Tourism of the People's Republic of China on Cultural and Tourism Development in 2024 ：汉英对照 / 中华人民共和国文化和旅游部编 . 北京 ：中国统计出版社，2025. 8. -- ISBN 978-7-5230-0745-7

Ⅰ. G12；F592

中国国家版本馆 CIP 数据核字第 2025TZ7483 号

中华人民共和国文化和旅游部 2024 年文化和旅游发展统计公报

作　　者／中华人民共和国文化和旅游部
责任编辑／张　怡
出版发行／中国统计出版社有限公司
通信地址／北京市丰台区西三环南路甲 6 号　邮政编码／100073
电　　话／邮购（010）63376909　书店（010）68783171
网　　址／http://www.zgtjcbs.com/
印　　刷／北京捷迅佳彩印刷有限公司
经　　销／新华书店
开　　本／880mm×1230mm　1/16
字　　数／50 千字
印　　张／2.25
版　　别／2025 年 8 月第 1 版
版　　次／2025 年 8 月第 1 次印刷
定　　价／28.00 元　28.00yuan(RMB)

目录

CONTENTS

中华人民共和国文化和旅游部
2024 年文化和旅游发展统计公报 [1]

2024 年，在以习近平同志为核心的党中央坚强领导下，全国文化和旅游系统坚持以习近平新时代中国特色社会主义思想为指导，全面贯彻落实党的二十大和二十届二中、三中全会精神，深入学习贯彻习近平文化思想，锚定建设文化强国、旅游强国目标，坚持稳中求进工作总基调，推动文化和旅游行业发展持续向好，扩内需、促消费、惠民生、助交流作用凸显，国家文化软实力和中华文化影响力进一步提升。

2024 年末，纳入统计报送范围的全国各类文化和旅游单位 [2]34.7 万个，从业人员 [3]463.1 万人。其中，各级文化和旅游行政部门所属单位 6.5 万个，从业人员 71.3 万人。

一、艺术创作生产繁荣活跃

2024 年，文化和旅游部深入实施 2023—2025 舞台艺术和美术创作行动计划、全国舞台艺术优秀节目创作扶持计划、国家主题性美术创作等各类艺术工程项目，遴选近 200 部（个、项）作品进行重点扶持，引导全国各地加强艺术创作、提升原创能力、推出艺术精品。国家艺术基金投入约 5.9 亿元，资助 793 个项目。组织举办第十届中国京剧艺术节、第九届中国昆曲艺术节、纪念西南剧展 80 周年暨第八届全国话剧优秀剧目展演、第三届全国曲艺木偶皮影优秀作品展演、戏曲百戏（昆山）盛典、首届全国小戏小品展演、第八届中国戏曲文化周、第二届全国民族器乐展演、“与时代同行与人民同心”——新时代优秀舞台艺术作品展演、国家艺术院团演出演播季、“美在荟萃——全国美术馆珍藏作品汇展”等展演展览活动，丰富群众精神文化生活。启动实施“聚光计划——抖音直播基层院团扶持专项”，截至 2024 年末，共有 88 家艺术院团 825 名演员（演奏员）入驻平台，直播超过 2.3 万场。

2024 年末，全国共有艺术表演团体 [4]2.2 万个，从业人员 41.9 万人。其中，文化和旅游部门所属艺术表演团体 1890 个，从业人员 10.4 万人。全年共演出 38.5 万场，国内观众 3.1 亿人次，演出收入 37.7 亿元。

2024 年末，全国共有艺术表演场馆 3516 个。其中，文化和旅游部门所属艺术表演场馆 1010 个，观众座席数 99.9 万个。全年共开展艺术演出 10.5 万场，观众 5248.6 万人次。

2024 年末，全国共有公共美术馆[5]723 个，从业人员 6465 人。全年共举办展览 1.1 万场，同比增长 9.3%，参观人次 7209.1 万人次，同比增长 15.9%。

二、公共文化服务体系更加完善

2024 年，文化和旅游部持续推进全国智慧图书馆体系和公共文化云项目建设，进一步提升公共数字文化服务水平。开展新型公共文化空间建设推广以及公共图书馆、文化馆服务宣传周等活动。举办公共图书馆视障阅读交流活动，保障视障群体阅读权益。组织“童书漂流”交流推广活动，丰富农村地区基层少年儿童阅读资源。举办首届中国新疆民间艺术季，实施“春雨工程”——文化和旅游志愿服务边疆行计划，有效促进各民族交往交流交融。组织“大地欢歌”全国乡村文化建设年、“四季村晚”“歌唱祖国”大家唱群众歌咏活动、全国广场舞展演、全国优秀群众文艺团队展演等活动，进一步丰富优秀文化供给。

（一）公共图书馆方面

2024 年末，全国共有公共图书馆[6]3248 个，从业人员 6.1 万人。其中，具有高级职称人员 0.8 万人，占 13.2%；具有中级职称人员 1.9 万人，占 31%。

图 1 2014—2024 年全国公共图书馆人均资源情况

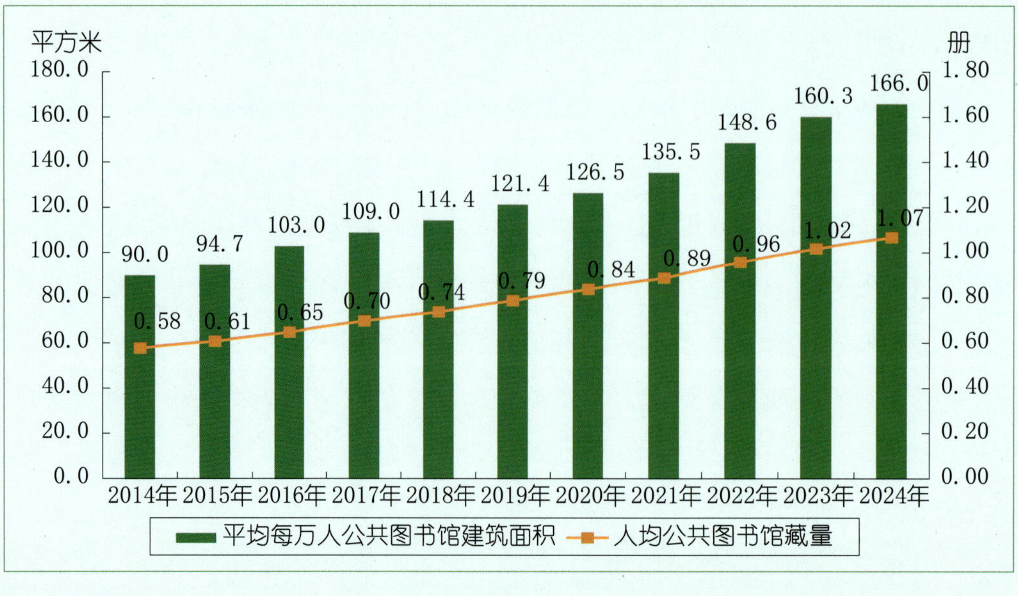

2024 年末，全国公共图书馆实际使用房屋建筑面积 2337.2 万平方米，同比增长 3.4%；全国图书总藏量[7]15 亿册，同比增长 4.8%；阅览室座席数 176.6 万个，同比增长 5.1%。

2024 年末，全国平均每万人公共图书馆建筑面积 166 平方米，比上年末增加 5.7 平方米；全国人均图书藏量 1.07 册，比上年末增加 0.05 册；全年全国人均购书费 1.5 元，与上年基本持平。

全年公共图书馆总流通人次[8]13.4 亿人次，同比增长 15.8%；书刊文献外借册次 8.4 亿册次，同比增长 7.0%；外借人次 3.6 亿人次，同比增长 7.7%。全年共为读者举办各种活动 33.2 万次，同比增长 13.0%；参加人次 2.6 亿人次，同比增长 20.2%。

图 2 2014—2024 年全国公共图书馆总流通人次及书刊外借册次

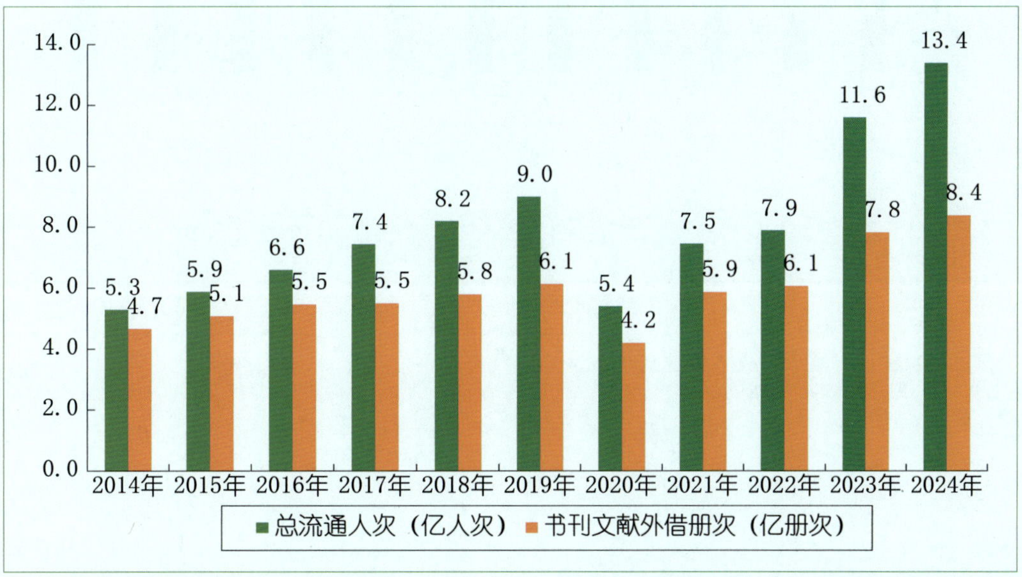

（二）**群众文化机构方面**

2024 年末，全国共有群众文化机构[9]4.4 万个，从业人员 19.6 万人。其中，具有高级职称的人员 0.8 万人，占 4.2%；具有中级职称人员 1.8 万人，占 9.3%。

2024 年末，全国群众文化机构实际使用房屋建筑面积 5562.3 万平方米，同比下降 1.2%。年末全国平均每万人群众文化设施建筑面积 395.0 平方米，同比下降 1.1%。

全年全国群众文化机构共组织开展各类文化活动[10]440 万场，同比增长 6.9%；服务 22 亿人次，同比增长 19.8%。

2024 年末，全国群众文化机构共有馆办文艺团体[11]10692 个，全年演出 15.3 万场，观众 9212.2 万人次。

图 3 2014-2024 年全国平均每万人群众文化设施建筑面积

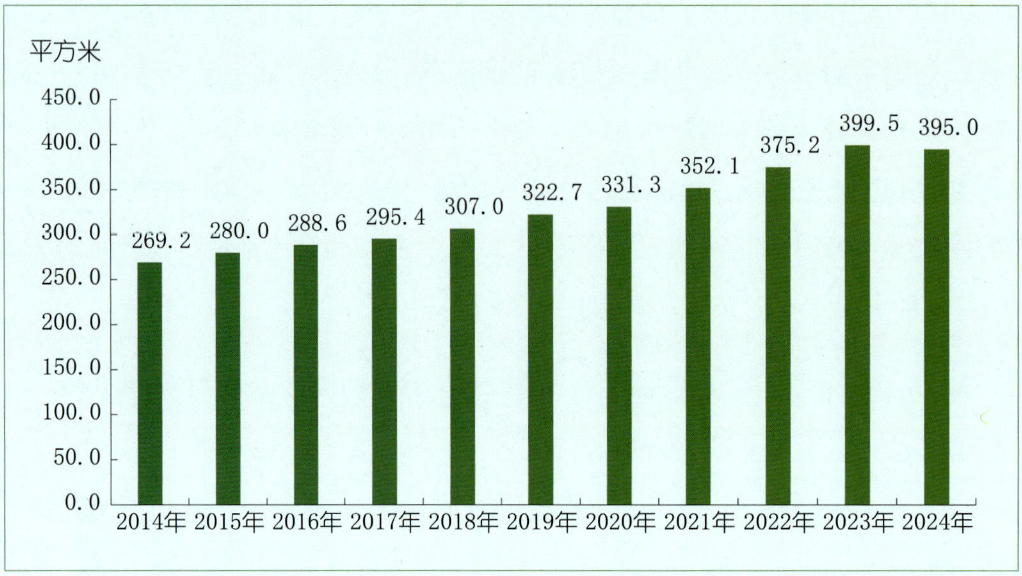

表 1 2024 年全国群众文化机构活动开展情况

项　目	总量		同比增长（%）	
	活动次数（万场次）	服务人次（亿人次）	活动次数	服务人次
各项活动总计	440	22.0	6.9	19.8
其中：文艺活动	254	16.5	3.1	18.8
训练班	152	1.2	12.9	14.8
展览	28	4.1	11.1	26.2
公益性讲座	7	0.1	11.2	0.4

三、文化遗产保护传承取得实效

（一）文物保护利用方面

2024 年，文化和旅游部、国家文物局全面加强文物保护利用工作，开展第四次全国文物普查，取得重要成果。推进文物建筑保护，实施廊桥行动计划，加强石窟寺、革命文物等保护，实施重点文物保护修缮项目。“北京中轴线——中国理想都城秩序的杰作”申遗成功，我国世界遗产总数达 59 项。组织实施打击防范文物犯罪专项行动、文物行业安全生产治本攻坚三年行动。持续推进开展中华文明探源工程和“考古中国”重大项目，启动夏商文明研究工程，二里头、武王墩和南海深海考古等工作取得重大进展。实施全国考古人才振兴计划。加强考古遗址展示利用。加强国家文物保护利用示范区建设。推进中国特色世界一流博物馆建设。持续提升博物馆开放服务水平。组织国际博物馆日、文化和自然遗产日等主题活动。加快古籍数字化整理和中华古籍智慧化服务平台建设。

2024 年末，全国共有文物行政主管部门、文物保护管理机构、国有博物馆、文物保护科研机构、其他文物事业机构和文物企业等各类文物机构 9716 个，从业人员 17.9 万人，其中高级职称 1.3 万人，占 7.3%；中级职称 2.4 万人，占 13.4%。

2024 年末，全国文物机构藏品 5082.8 万件／套，其中，国有博物馆藏品 4233.3 万件／套，占藏品总量的 83.3%。

2024 年，全国文物机构共举办陈列展览 3 万个，其中，基本陈列[12]1.3 万个，临时展览[13]1.7 万个。接待观众 15.5 亿人次，同比增长 10.3%，其中未成年人 3.5 亿人次，同比增长 9.6%，占参观总人数的 22.6%。国有博物馆接待观众 13.3 亿人次，同比增长 11.2%，占文物机构接待观众总数的 85.8%。

图 4 2014—2024 年全国文物机构接待观众人次及未成年人观众人次

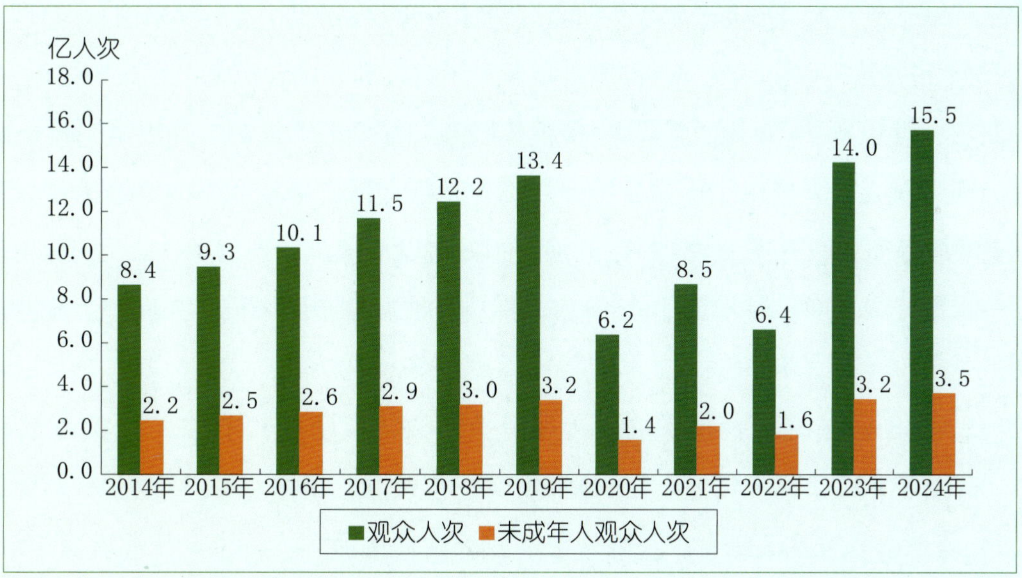

（二）非物质文化遗产保护传承方面

2024 年，文化和旅游部扎实推进非遗系统性保护。“春节——中国人庆祝传统新年的社会实践”项目成功列入人类非物质文化遗产代表作名录，“羌年”等 3 个项目成功从急需保护的非物质文化遗产名录转入人类非物质文化遗产代表作名录。推动国家级文化生态保护区建设。实施黄河流域、大运河、长城非遗保护传承弘扬行动计划。推进传统工艺高质量发展。推进第六批国家级非物质文化遗产代表性传承人认定工作。开展国家级非物质文化遗产代表性传承人传承活动评估。表彰全国非物质文化遗产保护工作 100 个先进集体和 198 名先进个人。深入实施中国非物质文化遗产传承人研修培训计划，支持 105 所院校开展 118 期研修班，培训学员 3280 人次。公布 99 家国家级非物质文化遗产生产性保护示范基地。加强非遗工坊建设，截至 2024 年末，全国共建有非遗工坊 1.1 万家。

举办中国非遗博览会、“新疆是个好地方”对口援疆非遗展示、“茶和天下 共享非遗”“非遗融入现代生活”主题活动和非遗购物节，组织中国非遗保护实践主题展、云游非遗影像展等展览活动。开展“文化和自然遗产日”非遗宣传展示活动 1.2 万余场、春节非遗宣传展示活动 4.5 万场。

2024 年末，全国共有国家级非物质文化遗产代表性项目 1557 项，国家级非物质文化遗产代表性传承人 3056 名。列入联合国教科文组织非物质文化遗产名录、名册项目 44 个。

2024 年末，全国共有非物质文化遗产保护机构 2397 个，从业人员 1.7 万人。全年全国各类非物质文化遗产保护机构举办演出 8 万场，同比下降 2.3%；举办民俗活动 2.1 万场，同比增长 17.2%；举办展览 2.2 万场，同比增长 2.3%。

四、文化和旅游市场规范有序

2024 年，文化和旅游部持续优化营商环境，文化和旅游市场发展规范有序。实施《国内旅游提升计划（2023—2025 年）》，推进旅游服务质量评价体系建设。举办“5 · 19 中国旅游日”系列活动，推出 6300 余条惠民措施。修订印发《导游服务规范》国家标准，出台《电子竞技场馆运营服务规范》国家标准。实现行政审批“一网通办”，完善政务服务“好差评”机制，开展第二批全国互联网上网服务行业云服务试点，完成电子证照应用试点工作。指导演出新空间、网络演出剧（节）目、剧本娱乐、电竞酒店等新业态有序发展。持续开展信用经济发展试点工作，举办“文明旅游 美丽中国”系列活动，培育国家级文明旅游示范单位 46 家。部署开展文化市场未成年人保护、旅游市场秩序专项整治行动。

2024 年末，全国通过统计直报系统报送和审核的文化市场经营单位[14]19.2 万家，从业人员 128.5 万人，营业收入 21210.4 亿元，营业利润 1345.1 亿元。其中，娱乐场所 5.3 万个，从业人员 43.3 万人，营业收入 874.2 亿元。互联网上网服务营业场所 8.3 万个，从业人员 16.4 万人，营业收入 179.3 亿元，营业利润 23.9 亿元。演出市场单位 3.5 万个，从业人员 47.8 万人，营业收入 9214.5 亿元，营业利润 597.7 亿元。艺术品经营机构 0.8 万个，从业人员 2 万人，营业收入 580.6 亿元，营业利润 31.5 亿元。经营性互联网文化单位 1.2 万家，从业人员 19.1 万人，营业收入 10361.7 亿元，营业利润 700.1 亿元。

五、文化产业和旅游业活力迸发

2024 年，文化和旅游部持续推动文化产业和旅游业发展，促进文旅产业数字化转型升级，培育旅游演艺、数字演艺、线上演播、沉浸式体验等新型业态，开展数字赋能文旅场景建设行动，推动文旅产业赋能城市发展。持续实施文化产业赋能乡村振兴计划，开展文化产业赋能乡村振兴试点。新命名 219 家文化企业为国家文化产业示范基地，现有示范基地总数达 384 家。组织开展 5 期“多

彩中国 佳节好物”文化和旅游贸易促进活动，在中东、东南亚、欧洲等重点及新兴市场创新开展服务重点企业重点项目海外交流对接活动。举办中日韩文化产业论坛、中国（深圳）国际文化产业博览交易会等。举办中国文化旅游产业博览会，汇聚 2000 多家企业参展参会，成交额 3.85 亿元，项目签约额 300 多亿元。

推进实施《关于释放旅游消费潜力推动旅游业高质量发展的若干措施》，制定促进服务消费、冰雪经济、进一步培育新增长点繁荣文化和旅游消费的若干措施等政策。印发智慧旅游创新发展行动计划、推进旅游公路高质量发展五年行动方案。新增 102 个国家级夜间文化和旅游消费集聚区。开展全国文化和旅游消费促进活动。开展“旅游中国 美好生活”全国旅游宣传推广活动，举办“读苏轼 游神州”中华文化主题旅游线路宣传推广活动，开展“跟着演出去旅行”“跟着赛事去旅行”“跟着影视去旅行”品牌建设。组织“乡村创意生活季”“游购乡村”、旅游专列援疆援藏等活动。深入实施旅游促进各民族交往交流交融计划，遴选确定 38 个试点项目。实施旅游景区强基焕新行动、乡村旅游提质增效行动。举办“天工开物”2024 年工业旅游推广活动。发布“乡村四时好风光”、全国冰雪旅游等精品线路。新评定国家 5A 级旅游景区 19 家、国家级旅游度假区 22 个、国家级滑雪旅游度假地 7 个，推出 42 个智慧旅游沉浸式体验新空间培育试点项目。推荐云南阿者科村等 7 个乡村入选联合国旅游组织“最佳旅游乡村”。推进旅游厕所建设管理，旅游公共服务水平稳步提升。

据国家统计局统计，2024 年，全国规模以上文化及相关产业企业实现营业收入 141510 亿元，同比增长 6.0%。

2024 年末，全国共有 A 级旅游景区 16541 个，直接从业人员 165.3 万人，全年接待游客 67.6 亿人次，总收入 4814.2 亿元。

2024 年末，全国共有星级饭店 7716 家。根据全国旅游监管服务平台数据显示，全年全国星级饭店营业收入 1557.3 亿元，平均房价 371.7 元／间夜，平均出租率 49.2%。

2024 年末，全国共有旅行社 64616 家。根据旅行社填报系统数据显示，全年全国旅行社营业收入 5657.7 亿元，营业利润 37.8 亿元。

2024 年，国内居民出游 56.2 亿人次，同比增长 14.8%。其中，城镇居民国内出游 43.7 亿人次，同比增长 16.3%；农村居民国内出游 12.5 亿人次，同比增长 9.9%。国内居民出游总花费 5.8 万亿元，同比增长 17.1%。其中，城镇居民出游花费 4.9 万亿元，同比增长 18.0%；农村居民出游花费 0.8 万亿元，同比增长 12.2%。

2024 年，入境游客 13190.2 万人次，同比增长 60.8%。其中，外国游客入境 2694 万人次，同比增长 95.5%；中国香港、中国澳门和中国台湾居民入境 10496.2 万人次，同比增长 53.8%。内地居民出境旅游 12279.2 万人次，同比增长 41%。

图 5 2014—2024 年国内旅游发展情况

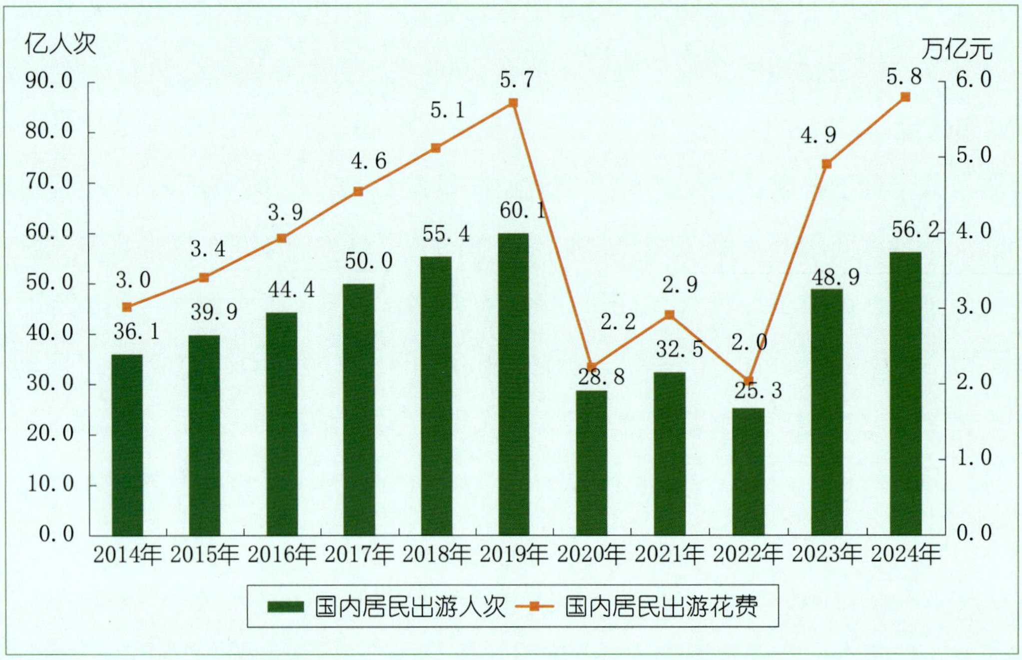

六、科技教育水平稳步提升

2024 年，文化和旅游部落实国家文化数字化战略、实施国家重点研发计划“文化科技与现代服务业”专项。实施文化和旅游科技创新研发、重点实验室资助项目 30 项。完成首批 11 个技术创新中心建设。会同工业和信息化部遴选公布全国文化和旅游装备技术提升优秀案例 47 个。出台旅游国际标准 1 项、文化和旅游国家标准及行业标准 21 项。推动艺术学“三大体系”建设，立项国家社科基金艺术学重大项目 17 个、年度项目 255 个。深化高校共建工作，实施文化艺术和旅游职业教育提质培优行动计划项目 60 个。举办全国文化艺术和旅游职业教育课程思政展示活动、第八届全国青少年民族器乐教育教学成果展示活动和第十三届“桃李杯”全国青少年舞蹈教育教学成果全国巡演等活动。

七、对外和对港澳台交流合作不断深入

2024 年，文化和旅游部积极践行全球文明倡议，组织中法文化旅游年、中美旅游高层对话、中柬人文交流年、中朝友好年、中坦旅游文化年、中赞文化和旅游年等大型活动，举办中俄文化年开幕式暨庆祝中俄建交 75 周年专场音乐会、中非合作论坛峰会文艺演出和普契尼音乐会等主场外交文艺演出，有力促进人文交流、民心相通。 出台实施《入境旅游促进计划（2024—2026 年）》，推动入境旅游便利化水平大幅提升，加强“你好！中国”国家旅游形象海外推广，举办中国国际旅游交易会。组织“良渚论坛”“欢乐春节”“茶和天下 · 雅集”“兰亭 · 雅集”“天涯共此时——中秋诗会”“发现中国之美”等系列活动。完善丝绸之路六大联盟机制，举办“艺汇丝路”采风作品展。

推进粤港澳大湾区文化和旅游发展，支持香港打造中外文化艺术交流中心、澳门打造世界旅游休闲中心。开展港澳大学生文化实践活动，举办“濠江月明夜”“国家艺术院团（澳门）演出季”“情系中华”等品牌活动。进一步推动对台文化和旅游交流，恢复福建居民赴金门、马祖旅游。

2024 年末，在全球共设有 50 家海外中国文化中心、20 家驻外旅游办事处。此外，在香港设有亚洲旅游交流中心，在台湾设有海峡两岸旅游交流协会台北办事处、高雄办事分处。

八、财政资金投入持续优化

2024 年，全国文化和旅游事业费[15]1216.2 亿元，比上年减少 64.1 亿元，同比下降 5%；全国人均文化和旅游事业费 86.4 元，比上年减少 4.5 元，同比下降 4.9%。文化和旅游事业费占财政总支出的比重为 0.43%，比上年下降 0.04 个百分点。

图 6 2014—2024 年人均文化和旅游事业费及增速情况

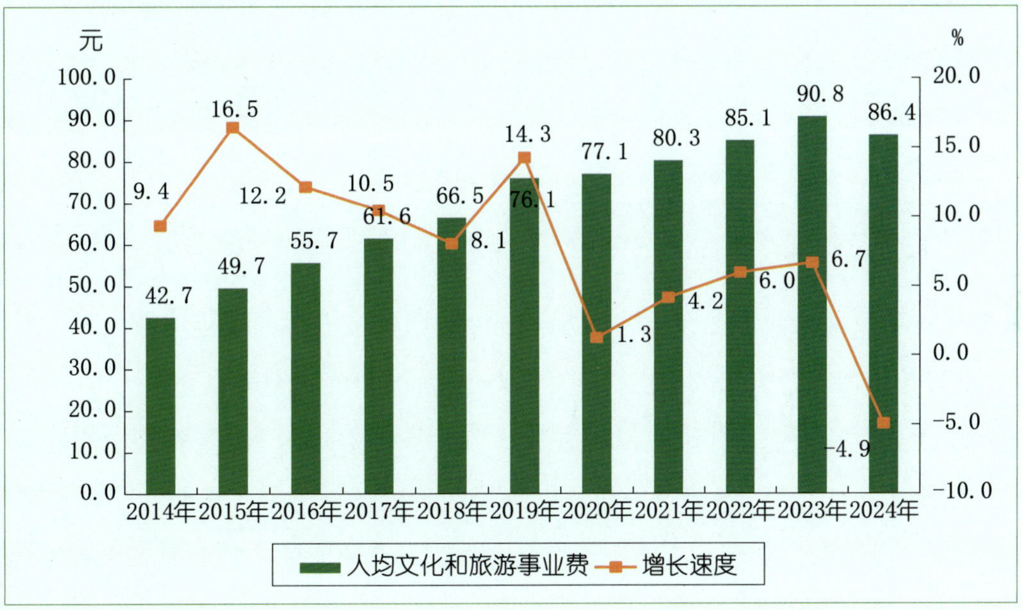

全国文化和旅游事业费中，县级以上文化和旅游事业费 565.8 亿元，占 46.5%，比重比上年下降了 0.1 个百分点；县级及县级以下文化和旅游事业费 650.4 亿元，占 53.5%，比重比上年提升了 0.1 个百分点。东部地区[16]文化和旅游事业费 521.8 亿元，占 42.9%，比重比上年下降了 0.8 个百分点。中部地区文化和旅游事业费 315.8 亿元，占 26%，比重比上年提高了 0.7 个百分点。西部地区文化和旅游事业费 344 亿元，占 28.3%，比重比上年下降了 0.4 个百分点。

表 2 全国文化和旅游事业费按城乡和区域分布情况

项目		2005 年	2010 年	2015 年	2020 年	2023 年	2024 年
总量（亿元）	全国	133.8	323.1	686.0	1088.3	1280.4	1216.2
	# 县级以上	98.1	206.7	352.8	501.0	597.6	565.8
	县级及县以下	35.7	116.4	330.1	587.3	682.7	650.4
	# 东部地区	64.4	143.4	287.9	491.6	560.0	521.8
	中部地区	30.6	78.7	164.3	269.8	324.1	315.8
	西部地区	27.6	85.8	193.9	301.6	367.4	344.0
所占比重（%）	全国	100.0	100.0	100.0	100.0	100.0	100.0
	# 县级以上	73.3	64.0	51.7	46.0	46.7	46.5
	县级及县以下	26.7	36.0	48.3	54.0	53.3	53.5
	# 东部地区	48.1	44.4	42.1	45.1	43.7	42.9
	中部地区	22.9	24.3	24.1	24.8	25.3	26.0
	西部地区	20.6	26.6	28.4	27.7	28.7	28.3

注释：

[1] 本公报中各项数据为初步统计数据。各项统计数据均未包括香港特别行政区、澳门特别行政区和台湾省。部分数据因四舍五入的原因，存在着与分项合计不等的情况。

[2] 文化和旅游单位是指全国各级文化和旅游部门主办的或实行行业管理的文化机构，不含各级新闻出版、广播影视等部门主办或管理的机构。根据现行的统计制度，各级文化和旅游部门主办单位（如公共图书馆、文化馆、文化站、博物馆、公有制艺术表演团体、公有制艺术表演场馆等）全部纳入统计范围。实行行业管理的文化和旅游单位中，包括娱乐场所和互联网上网服务营业场所、非公有制艺术表演团体、非公有制艺术表演场馆、经营性互联网文化单位、艺术品经营机构和演出经纪机构和 A 级景区、星级饭店和旅行社数据。

[3] 从业人员是指各级文化和旅游部门主办或实行行业管理的机构中工作并取得劳动报酬的人员。

[4] 艺术表演团体指由文化和旅游部门主办或实行行业管理（经文化和旅游行政部门审批并领取营业性演出许可证），专门从事表演艺术等活动的各类专业艺术表演团体，含民间职业剧团（不包括群众业余文艺表演团队）。

[5] 美术馆是指由文化和旅游部门主办或实行行业管理的，具备展览、典藏、研究及公共教育和服务功能的、向公众开放的国有美术馆；以及在民政部门登记注册并在文化和旅游部门备案的，具

备展览、典藏、研究及公共教育和服务功能的、向公众开放的、非营利性的民营美术馆。

[6] 公共图书馆是指文化和旅游部门主办的面向社会服务的图书馆。

[7] 公共图书馆总藏量指本馆已编目的古籍、图书、期刊和报纸的合订本、小册子、手稿，以及缩微制品、录像带、录音带、光盘等视听文献资料数量之和。

[8] 公共图书馆总流通人次是指本年度内到图书馆场馆接受图书馆服务的总人次，包括借阅书刊、咨询问题，以及参加各类读者活动等。

[9] 群众文化机构是指各级文化和旅游部门主办的开展群众文化活动的场所，主要包括文化馆（含综合性文化中心、群众艺术馆）、文化站。

[10] 群众文化机构组织开展活动是指组织文艺活动、举办训练班、举办展览和组织公益性讲座的总和。

[11] 群众文化机构馆办文艺团体是指由本馆人员组成的为群众提供文艺演出的演出团队。

[12] 基本陈列指在本馆布置陈列、地点固定、时间较长的展出。

[13] 临时展览指在本机构内设置，由本馆设计布陈，形式比较多样的展出。

[14] 文化市场经营单位是指经审批或备案并领取相关许可或备案文件的、从事文化经营和文化服务活动的机构。按照现行统计制度，文化市场经营单位统计范围包括娱乐场所和互联网上网服务营业场所、非公有制艺术表演团体、非公有制艺术表演场馆、经营性互联网文化单位、艺术品经营机构和演出经纪机构。

[15] 文化和旅游事业费是指区域内各级财政对文化和旅游系统主办单位的经费投入总和。根据现行统计口径，文化和旅游事业费不包括各级文化和旅游行政部门的行政运行经费。

[16] 东部地区包括北京、天津、辽宁、上海、江苏、浙江、福建、山东、广东；中部地区包括河北、山西、吉林、黑龙江、安徽、江西、河南、湖北、湖南、海南；西部地区包括内蒙古、广西、重庆、四川、贵州、云南、西藏、陕西、甘肃、青海、宁夏、新疆。

Statistical Communiqué of the Ministry of Culture and Tourism of the People's Republic of China on Cultural and Tourism Development in 2024[1]

In 2024, under the firm leadership of the Central Committee of the Communist Party of China with Comrade Xi Jinping at its core, China’s cultural and tourism administrations, guided by Xi Jinping Thought on Socialism with Chinese Characteristics for A New Era, implemented the guiding principles from the Party's 20th National Congress and its 2nd and 3rd plenary sessions, gained a good understanding of Xi Jinping Thought on Culture and acted on it, set our goal at building acountry with vibrant culture and resilient tourism, stuck to the general principle of pursuing progress while ensuring stability, and promoted the sustainable and steady growth of cultural and tourism sectors, contributing steady economic growth and consumer spending as well as creating more jobs for the benefit of our people. China's cultural soft power and the international influence of Chinese culture have increased significantly.

347,000 national cultural and tourism units[2] with 4.631 million employees were brought into the statistical range by the end of 2024. Among them, 65,000 were affiliated to cultural and tourism authorities at different levels, which hired 713,000 employees[3].

I. A vibrant arts scene

In 2024, the Ministry of Culture and Tourism further implemented the 2023–2025 Performing Arts and Fine Arts Creation Action Plan, the national support plan for excellent performing arts programs, the national thematic fine arts supporting program, and various other arts projects. Around 200 works (pieces, items, projects) were selected for key support as role models to inspire outstanding artistic works and originality across the country. The National Arts Fund invested about 590 million yuan, supporting 793 projects. The Ministry organized and held a series of cultural and artistic events to enrich the public's spiritual and cultural life, including the 10th China Peking Opera Festival, the 9th China Kunqu Opera Festival, the 80th Anniversary Commemoration of the Southwest Drama Exhibition and the 8th National Excellent Drama Showcase, the 3rd National Quyi, Puppet, and Shadow Play Outstanding Works Showcase, the xiqu gala (Kunshan), the 1st National Small Drama and Sketch Showcase, the 8th China Xiqu Culture Week, the 2nd National Ethnic Instrumental Music Showcase, outstanding performing arts showcase in the new era, the National Art Troupes Performance and Broadcast Season, Exhibition of fine art works collected in art museums across the country. The Ministry also launched and implemented the "Spotlight Plan" — a Tiktok live-streaming support project for grassroots art troupes. By the end of 2024, a total of 88 art troupes and 825 performers (musicians) had joined the platform, streaming over 23,000 live sessions.

By the end of 2024, the number of art performance troupes[4] in China reached 22,000, with 419,000 professionals. Among them, there were 1,890 troupes affiliated with the Ministry of Culture and Tourism, employing 104,000 people. All art troupes in China presented 385,000 performances throughout the year, attracting 310 million domestic audience attendances. The total performing arts box office revenue was 3.77 billion yuan.

By the end of 2024, the number of performing arts venues in China amounted to 3,516, including 1,010 venues affiliated with the Ministry of Culture and Tourism, with a total of 999,000 seats. A total of 105,000 art performances were held in these venues throughout the year, with 52.486 million audience attendances.

By the end of 2024, there were 723 public art museums[5] in China with 6,465 employees. A total of 11,000 exhibitions were held throughout the year, a year-on-year increase of 9.3%, attracting 72.091 million visits, up 15.9% from the previous year.

II. An increasingly improved public service system

In 2024, the Ministry of Culture and Tourism advanced the development of a nationwide smart library system and the project of building cloud cultural database for public use, further enhancing public digital cultural services. Efforts were made to promote the development of new types of public cultural spaces, as well as to organize activities such as Public Library and Cultural Center Service Promotion Week. Reading and talking events for the visually impaired were held at public libraries to safeguard the reading rights of the visually impaired community. The children's books exchange and promotion campaign was organized to enrich reading resources for children and teenagers in rural areas. The First China Xinjiang Folk Art Season was held, and The "Spring Rain Project", a cultural and tourism volunteer service initiative tailored to border regions was implemented to effectively promote interactions, exchanges, and integration among all ethnic groups. Moreover, the Ministry launched a series of community cultural activities, including the all-year-long village gala series, vocal artists talent shows, public square dance galas and the tour and gala show of outstanding amateur art troupes to further enrich the supply of quality culture.

(1) Public libraries

By the end of 2024, there were in total 3,248 public libraries[6] nationwide, with 61,000 employees. Among them, 8,000 owned senior professional titles, accounting for 13.2%, and 19,000 owned medium-level professional titles, accounting for 31%.

According to statistics at the end of 2024, the actual floor space used by public library buildings totaled 233.72 million square meters, up by 3.4% over the end of the previous year. 1.5 billion books[7] were collected in these libraries, up by 4.8%. The number of seats in reading rooms was 1.766 million, up by 5.1%.

By the end of 2024, the floor space of public libraries for each ten thousand persons was 166 square meters, an increase of 5.7 square meters over the end of the previous year; the number of books per capita was 1.07, an increase of 0.05 over the previous year; the money spent on books per capita was 1.5 yuan, basically the same as that of the previous year.

Figure 1: Public library resources per capita (2014-2024)

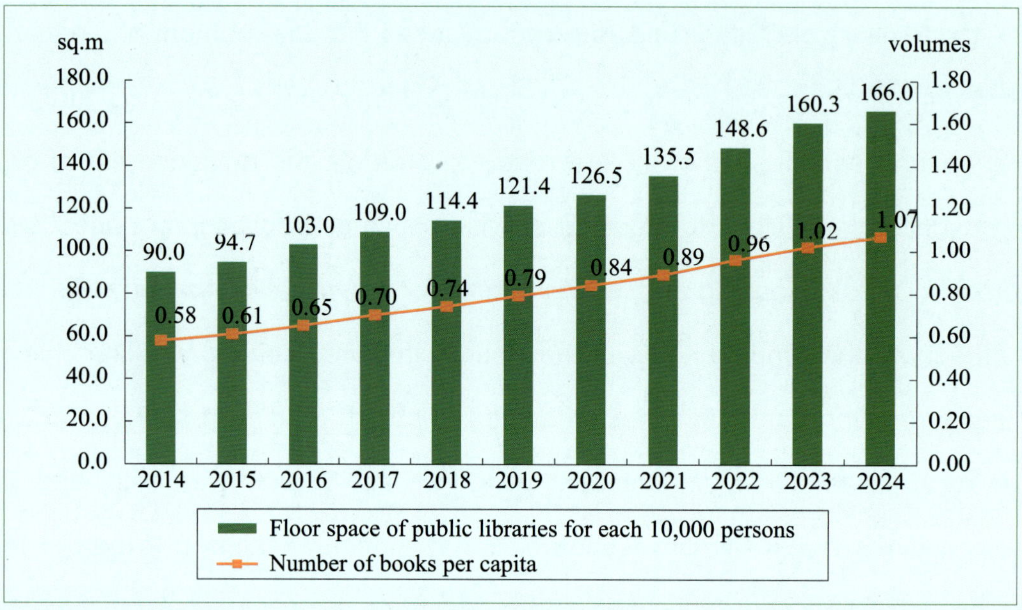

In 2024, the total number of visits[8] made by the people to public libraries reached 1.34 billion, an increase of 15.8%. The total number of books, magazines, and documents borrowed by readers reached 840 million copies, up by 7.0%; readers borrowed books for a total of 360 million times, an increase of 7.7% over the previous year. The number of various activities organized for readers totaled 332,000, up by 13.0%, which attracted 260 million attendances, an increase of 20.2%.

Figure 2: Total number of visits of Chinese people to public libraries and books borrowed (2014-2024)

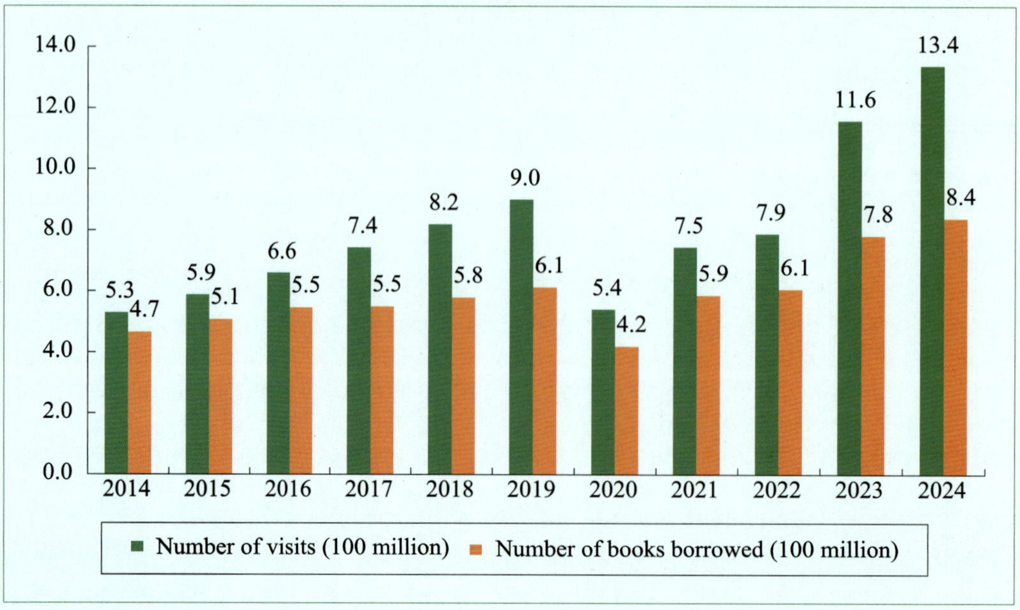

(2) Public and community cultural institutions

By the end of 2024, there were a total of 44,000 public and community cultural institutions[9] across the country. The total number of employees in these institutions reached 196,000. Staff with senior professional titles numbered 8,000, accounting for 4.2% of the total, while staff with medium-grade professional titles totaled 18,000, accounting for 9.3%.

By the end of the year, the actual floor space used by public and community cultural institutions was 55.623 million square meters, down by 1.2% compared with the previous year. The average area covered by cultural facilities for every 10,000 people was 395.0 square meters, a decrease of 1.1% year-on-year.

Figure 3: Average floor space used by public and community cultural institutions per 10,000 persons (2014-2024)

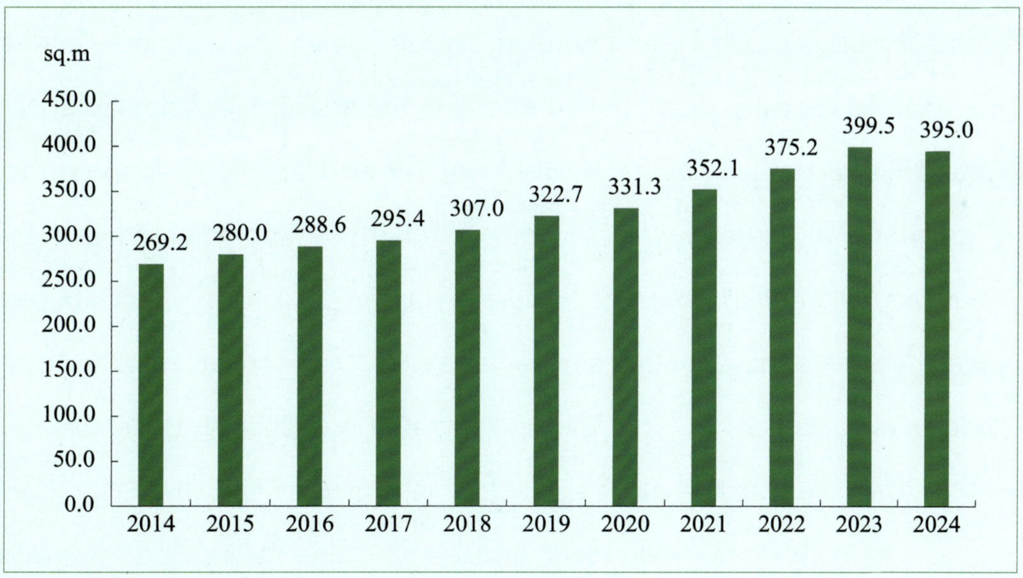

Throughout the year, public and community cultural institutions nationwide organized a total of 4.4 million cultural activities[10], an increase of 6.9% from the previous year, serving 2.2 billion person-times, up by 19.8%.

By the end of 2024, public and community cultural institutions nationwide hosted 10,692 cultural and arts groups[11] under cultural centers, which presented 153,000 performances to a total audience of 92.122 million.

Table 1: Activities carried out by public and community cultural institutions nationwide (2024)

Item	Total amount		Increased over previous year(%)	
	Number of events (10,000 shows)	Attendances (100 million person-times)	Number of events	Attendances
Total number of events	**440**	**22.0**	**6.9**	**19.8**
Art performances	254	16.5	3.1	18.8
Workshops	152	1.2	12.9	14.8
Exhibitions	28	4.1	11.1	26.2
Public lectures	7	0.1	11.2	0.4

III. Tangible achievements in cultural heritage protection

1. Stewardship of cultural heritage

In 2024, the Ministry of Culture and Tourism, together with the National Cultural Heritage Administration, comprehensively strengthened efforts in the stewardship of cultural heritage. The Fourth National Cultural Heritage Census was launched and achieved important results. The protection of architectural heritage was promoted through the implementation of the Covered Bridge Safeguarding Action Plan, while efforts were intensified to conserve rock-cut cave temples, revolution-related cultural relics, and other key heritage sites. Major cultural heritage protection and restoration projects were carried out. The "Beijing Central Axis: A Building Ensemble Exhibiting the Ideal Order of the Chinese Capital" was successfully inscribed on the UNESCO World Heritage List, bringing the total number of World Heritage sites in China to 59. Special taskforces were organized to combat and prevent crimes related to cultural relics, along with the three-year action plan for fundamentally improving safety production in the cultural relics sector. The Ministry continued advancing the project to trace the origins of Chinese civilization and the “Archaeology of China” initiative. The research project on the xia and shang dynasties’ civilization was launched, and significant progress was made in archaeological work at sites such as Erlitou, the tomb of King Wu, and deep-sea archaeology in the South China Sea.

An action plan to train more talents in archaeology was implemented, and more efforts were made to improve the public access of archaeological sites. More work was done to build national-level cultural heritage protection and utilization model zones. Progress continued in building world-class museums with Chinese characteristics, and the level of public access to museums and public services were continuously improved. Public awareness activities such as International Museum Day and Cultural and Natural Heritage Day were organized. The digitization of ancient books was accelerated, and the development of a smart service platform for Chinese ancient books was actively promoted.

By the end of 2024, there were 9,716 cultural heritage institutions all over China. Among these were administrative departments for cultural relics, heritage conservation and management institutions, state-owned museums, cultural relic protection research institutions, other public heritage service organizations, and heritage enterprises. The number of employees at cultural heritage institutions reached 179,000. Among them, 13,000 had senior professional titles, accounting for 7.3%; and 24,000 had medium-grade professional titles, accounting for 13.4%.

By the end of 2024, there were 50.828 million cultural relics (or sets of artifacts) in the collections of the cultural heritage institutions. Among these, the amount of items (sets) in state-owned museums totaled 42.333 million, which accounted for 83.3% of the total.

Figure 4: Total visits and visits made by people under the age of 18 to heritage institutions and museums across China(2014-2024)

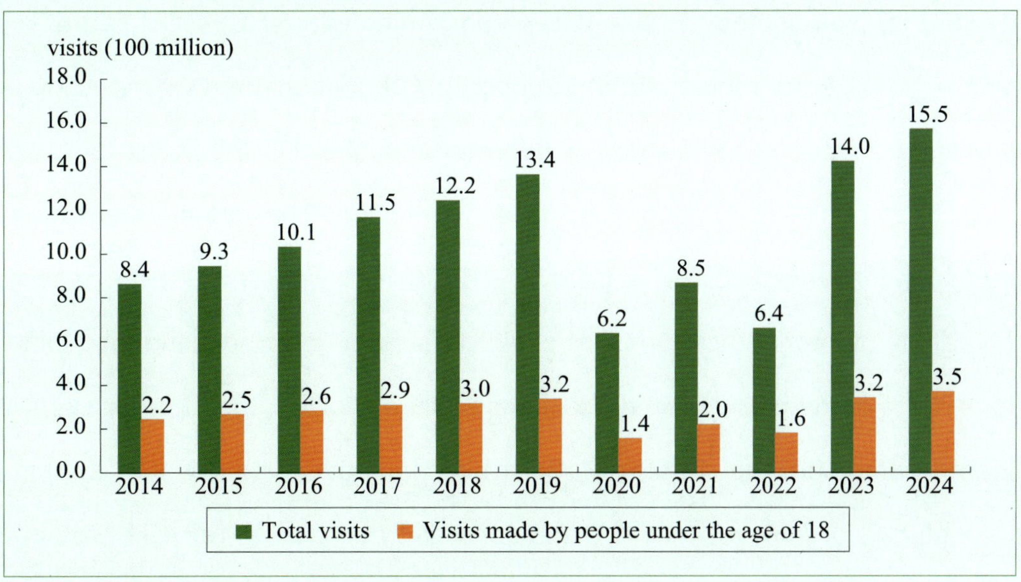

In 2024, a total of 30,000 exhibitions were held by various cultural heritage institutions across the country. Among these, 13,000 were permanent exhibitions[12], and 17,000 were temporary exhibitions[13]. The total number of visitors reached 1.55 billion, an increase of 10.3% compared to the previous year. Among the visitors, 350 million were minors, an increase of 9.6%, accounting for 22.6% of all visitors. State-owned museums received 1.33 billion visitors, an increase of 11.2%, accounting for 85.8% of the total number of visitors received by cultural heritage institutions.

2.Intangible cultural heritage (ICH) safeguarding

In 2024, the Ministry of Culture and Tourism made solid progress in the systematic protection of Intangible Cultural Heritage (ICH). “Spring Festival, social practices of the Chinese people in celebration of the traditional new year” was successfully inscribed on the Representative List of the Intangible Cultural Heritage of Humanity of UNESCO. In addition, three elements, including Qiang New Year festival, were successfully transferred from the List of Intangible Cultural Heritage in Need of Urgent Safeguarding to the Representative List. Efforts to promote the construction of national-level cultural reserves were advanced. The ICH safeguarding, transmission and promotion action plans for the Yellow River Basin, the Grand Canal, and the Great Wall were implemented. High-quality development of traditional craftsmanship was promoted. The recognition of the sixth batch of national-level ICH representative bearers was carried out, and evaluations of their transmission activities were conducted. 100 outstanding collectives and 198 outstanding individuals were commended for their contributions to ICH safeguarding efforts. The ICH bearer research and training program was further implemented, supporting 105 institutions in conducting 118 training sessions, providing a total of 3,280 training opportunities. A list of 99 national-level role model bases for production based ICH safeguarding was published. The development ICH workshops was promoted. By the end of 2024, a total of 11,000 ICH workshops had been established nationwide. A variety of themed activities and exhibitions were held, including the China ICH Expo, the “Xinjiang is a wonderful place” paired assistance ICH exhibition, the “Tea for Harmony: Shared Heritage” theme campaign, the “ICH in Modern Life” initiative, and the ICH shopping festival. Other efforts included organizing theme exhibitions such as the China ICH protection practice exhibition and the digital ICH exhibition. More than 12,000 ICH public awareness activities were organized during the Cultural and Natural Heritage Day, and over 45,000 such activities were held to celebrate the inscription of Spring Festival on the UNESCO Representative List.

By the end of 2024, there were 3,056 national-level representative intangible cultural heritage (ICH) bearers recognized by the Ministry of Culture and Tourism who were still alive and 1,557 national-level representative ICH elements endorsed by the State Council. There were 44 Chinese elements inscribed on the UNESCO Representative List of the Intangible Cultural Heritage of Humanity.

By the end of 2024, there were a total of 2,397 ICH safeguarding institutions across the country, with 17,000 employees. Throughout the year in the country, these institutions held 80,000 showcases, down by 2.3%, 21,000 folklore activities, up by 17.2%, and 22,000 exhibitions, up by 2.3%.

IV. Effective market regulation

In 2024, the Ministry of Culture and Tourism continued to optimize the business environment, ensuring that the cultural and tourism market developed in an orderly manner. It implemented the Domestic Tourism Promotion Plan (2023–2025) and advanced the development of a tourism service quality evaluation system. A series of themed events were organized for “China Tourism Day” on May 19, during which over 6,300 measures were launched to benefit consumers. The national standard known as the code of conduct for tour guide services was revised and published, and a new national standard for operation and service specifications for e-sports venues was introduced. Full implementation of “one-stop online administrative approval” was achieved, while the government service rating mechanism was further improved. The Ministry also launched the second batch of national digital service pilot programs for the internet access service industry and completed pilot projects for electronic certificate applications. It provided guidance for the orderly development of emerging businesses in the cultural and tourism sectors, including new types of performance spaces, online performance and theater productions, script-based entertainment, and e-sports hotels. The Ministry continued to carry out pilot programs for the development of a credit-based economy, and organized a campaign to advocate tourist etiquette, identifying 46 national-level role model institutions for responsible tourism. Additionally, targeted campaigns were launched to enhance the protection of minors in the cultural market and to strengthen order in the tourism market.

By the end of the year, business units in the nationwide cultural market[14] reached 192,000 according to data submitted by these units, with 1,285,000 employees and a revenue of 2,121.04 billion yuan. The profit was 134.51 billion yuan. Among them, there were 53,000 entertainment venues with 433,000 employees, generating 87.42 billion yuan in revenue. There were 83,000 internet cafés with 164,000 employees, generating 17.93 billion yuan in revenue and 2.39 billion yuan in profit. There were 35,000 performing arts companies with 478,000 employees, generating 921.45 billion yuan in revenue and 59.77 billion yuan in profit. There were 8,000 art dealers with 20,000 employees, generating 58.06 billion yuan in revenue and 3.15 billion yuan in profit. Business units engaged in internet cultural operations totaled 12,000, with 191,000 employees, generating 1,036.17 billion yuan in revenue and 70.01 billion yuan in profit.

V. Prosperous cultural industry and tourism

In 2024, the Ministry of Culture and Tourism continued to promote the development of the cultural and tourism industries, advancing the digital transformation and upgrading of the sectors. It fostered the growth of emerging businesses such as performing arts shows at tourist destinations, digital performances, online broadcasting, and immersive experiences. The Ministry also launched initiatives to digitally empower cultural and tourism consumption, further integrating cultural and tourism industries into urban development strategies. Efforts to support rural revitalization through cultural industries were sustained. The Ministry continued implementing a program to help revitalize rural areas with creativity and launched various pilot projects. A total of 219 cultural enterprises were newly designated as national cultural industry role model bases, bringing the total number to 384. To promote cultural and tourism trade, the Ministry organized five sessions of trade fairs to facilitate overseas exchange and B2B events for key enterprises and major projects in priority and emerging markets such as the Middle East, Southeast Asia, and Europe. The Ministry also hosted major international and national events, including the China-Japan-Korea Cultural Industry Forum, the China (Shenzhen) International Cultural Industries Fair, and the China Cultural and Tourism Industry Expo, which brought together more than 2,000 enterprises, with on-site transactions totaling 385 million yuan, and signed project contracts exceeding 30 billion yuan.

The Ministry implemented Several Measures to Stimulate Tourist Spending and Promote High-Quality Tourism Development. It also formulated supporting policies to promote service consumption, stimulate the ice and snow economy, and foster new growth points to encourage more spending on cultural and tourism products. Further strategic planning included the release of the Smart Tourism Innovation and Development Action Plan and the Five-Year Action Plan for the high-quality development of roads leading to destinations. During the year, 102 new national-level nighttime cultural and tourism consumption clusters were established, and nationwide cultural and tourism consumption promotion activities were carried out. The Ministry also launched a national tourism campaign, featuring a range of themed promotional activities. These included a program to promote travel routes associated with the cultural personality and poet Su Shi from ancient China, as well as brand events to promote destinations mentioned in or associated with entertainment shows, sports games, and films and TV shows. Several initiatives focused on rural tourism development and revitalization were implemented, including bazaars to promote rural products, and special train tours around Xinjiang and Xizang. To help strengthen solidarity and mutual exchange among all ethnic groups, the Ministry carried out a tourism promotion plan in ethnic areas, and selected 38 pilot projects under this initiative. It also launched action plans to strengthen the infrastructure and upgrade tourist destinations and to improve the experience in rural tourism. The 2024 industrial tourism promotion campaign was held to spotlight China's industry heritage. New themed tourism routes such as seasonal rural tours and ice and snow tours were released. 19 new sites were designated as national 5A-level tourist attractions, 22 sites were recognized as national-level tourist resorts, and 7 sites were rated as national-level ski tourism resorts. The Ministry also launched 42 pilot projects to foster smart tourism immersive experience spaces. Seven villages, including Azheke Village in Yunnan, were recognized as Best Tourism Villages in UNWTO's list. Public service infrastructure like toilets in destinations was improved.

According to the National Bureau of Statistics, in 2024, the total turnover of major cultural and culture-related businesses reached 14,151 billion yuan, increasing by 6.0% over that of the previous year.

By the end of this year, there were 16,541 A-level tourist sites in China, with 1.653 million employees. Their total revenue in 2024 reached 481.42 billion yuan, with total visits of 6.76 billion.

By the end of the year, there were in total 7,716 star hotels in China. According to the national tourism supervision service platform, their total sales in 2024 reached 155.73 billion yuan, with the average daily rate (ADR) of 371.7 yuan per room/night and the average occupancy rate of 49.2%.

By the end of 2024, travel agencies across the country reached 64,616. According to the statistics of the travel agency database, their total sales in 2024 reached 565.77 billion yuan, with a profit of 3.78 billion yuan.

Throughout the year, 5.62 billion domestic visits were made by Chinese tourists, an increase of 14.8% year-on-year. Among these, urban residents made 4.37 billion domestic trips, up by 16.3%, and rural residents made 1.25 billion domestic trips, up by 9.9%. Total spending by domestic tourists amounted to 5.8 trillion yuan, up by 17.1%. Of this, urban residents spent 4.9 trillion yuan, up by 18.0% year-on-year, and rural residents, 0.8 trillion yuan, up by 12.2%.

Figure 5: Domestic tourism development of China (2014-2024)

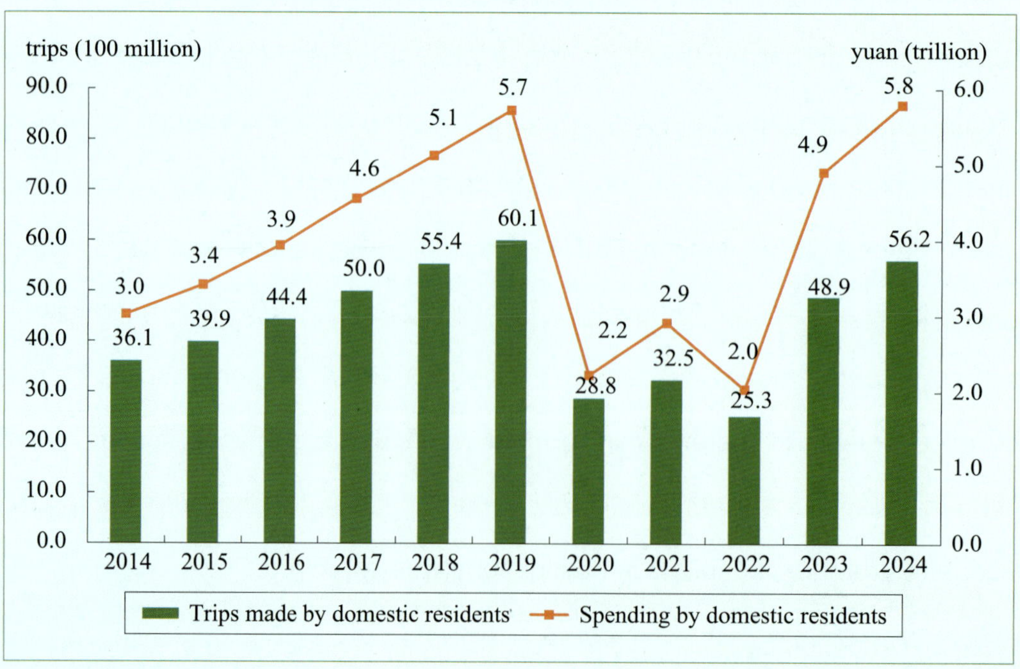

In 2024, China received 131.902 million inbound visits, a year-on-year increase of 60.8%. Among them, 26.94 million were made by foreigners, a 95.5% increase; and 104.962 million were made by compatriots from Hong Kong, Macao, and Taiwan, a 53.8% increase. Meanwhile, 122.792 million outbound trips were made by residents from the Chinese mainland, representing a 41% year-on-year increase.

VI. Further improvements of culture and tourism related education and technology

In 2024, the Ministry of Culture and Tourism put into practice the national strategy to digitize cultural contents and carried out the national key R&D program on culture, technology and modern service sector. A total of 30 projects were launched under the Ministry's initiatives to support technological innovation in culture and tourism and fund key laboratories. The construction of the first batch of 11 technology innovation centers was successfully completed. In collaboration with the Ministry of Industry and Information Technology, the Ministry identified and released 47 exemplary cases highlighting advances in cultural and tourism equipment and technology. The Ministry issued 1 international tourism standard, along with 21 national and industry standards in cultural and tourism sectors. Efforts to build the "three major systems" of Chinese art studies were further strengthened, and the Ministry initiated 17 major projects and 255 annual projects funded by the National Social Sciences Fund in the discipline of arts. To deepen partnerships with institutions of higher learning, the Ministry implemented 60 projects under the Action Plan to improve vocational education related to culture, arts, and tourism. In addition, the Ministry organized a range of national-level educational and cultural events, including an open classroom program on vocational education related to culture, arts and tourism, the 8th national showcase of achievements in youth ethnic instrumental music education, and the 13th "Taoli Cup" national tour of performances made by young and teenage dance award winners.

VII. Further exchanges and cooperation with foreign countries, Hong Kong, Macao, and Taiwan

In 2024, the Ministry of Culture and Tourism actively implemented the Global Civilization Initiative, organizing a series of large-scale events such as the China-France Year of Culture and

Tourism, China-U.S. high-level dialogue on tourism, China-Cambodia People-to-People Exchange Year, China-DPRK Year of Friendship, China-Tanzania Year of Tourism and Culture, and the China-Zambia Year of Culture and Tourism. The Ministry also hosted major diplomatic cultural performances, including the opening ceremony of the China-Russia year of culture and the special concert celebrating the 75th anniversary of diplomatic relations between China and Russia, the cultural performance for the Forum on China-Africa Cooperation (FOCAC) Summit, and the Puccini concert, which powerfully promoted people-to-people exchanges and mutual understanding between China and the world. The Inbound Tourism Promotion Plan (2024–2026) was launched and implemented to significantly facilitate China's inbound tourism. The "Nihao! China" Chinese tourism image campaign was carried out overseas, and the China International Travel Mart was successfully held. A series of events were organized, including the Liangzhu Forum, "Happy Chinese New Year", "Tea for Harmony: Yaji Cultural Salon", "Lanting: Cultural Salon", "A Mooment to Share: Mid-Autumn Festival", and "Discover China" tours. The mechanism of the six major Silk Road alliances was further improved, and the "Silk Road: Artists' Rendezvous" exhibition was held. Efforts were made to promote the cultural and tourism development of the Guangdong-Hong Kong-Macao Greater Bay Area, and we supported Hong Kong in becoming a center for cultural and artistic exchanges between China and the rest of the world, and Macao in developing into a world center for tourism and leisure. Cultural practice activities were organized for university students from Hong Kong and Macao, and key brand events were held such as "A Bright Moon over Macao", "Performing Season of National Art Troupes (Macao)", and art performances focusing on building bonds between Chinese mainland and Hong Kong and Macao. Further progress was made in promoting cross-strait cultural and tourism exchanges, including the resumption of travel permits for Fujian residents to Kinmen and Matsu.

By the end of 2024, there were a total of 50 overseas China Cultural Centers and 20 Chinese tourism offices in foreign countries. Moreover, the Asia Tourism Exchange Center was established in Hong Kong, and the offices of the Association for Tourism Exchange Across the Taiwan Straits were set up in both Taipei and Kaohsiung.

VIII. Stronger support from the central budget

The total amount of cultural and tourism undertaking expenses[15] for the whole year was 121.62 billion yuan, a decrease of 6.41 billion yuan compared with that of the previous year, down by 5% ; as for the national cultural and tourism undertaking expenses per capita, the total was 86.4 yuan, a decrease of 4.5 yuan compared with the previous year, down by 4.9%. Cultural and tourism undertaking expenses accounted for 0.43% of the state expenditure of China, a decrease of 0.04 percentage points from the previous year.

Figure 6: The total amount and growth rate of China's cultural and tourism undertaking expenses per capita(2014-2024)

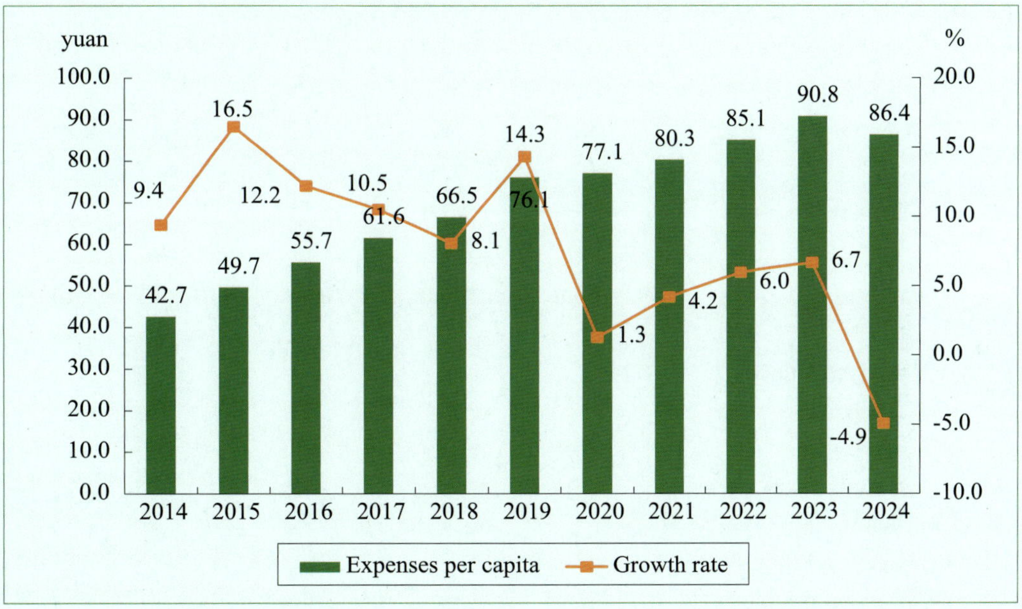

Regarding the national cultural and tourism undertaking expenses, that of cultural and tourism units above county level was 56.58 billion yuan , accounting for 46.5%, a decrease of 0.1 percentage points compared with the previous year; that of cultural and tourism units of county level or below the level of county was 65.04 billion yuan, accounting for 53.5%, an increase of 0.1 percentage points in the sense of its proportion. The cultural and tourism undertaking expenses of the eastern region[16] reached 52.18 billion yuan, accounting for 42.9%, and its proportion decreased by 0.8 percentage points; that of the central region reached 31.58 billion yuan, accounting for 26%, its proportion increased by 0.7 percentage points; and that of the western region reached 34.4 billion yuan , accounting for 28.3%, a decrease of 0.4 percentage points compared to the previous year.

Table 2: Distribution of cultural and tourism undertaking expenses of China

Item		In 2005	In 2010	In 2015	In 2020	In 2023	In 2024
Total Amount (100 million yuan)	**National**	**133.8**	**323.1**	**686.0**	**1088.3**	**1280.4**	**1216.2**
	# Above County level	98.1	206.7	352.8	501.0	597.6	565.8
	County-level and below	35.7	116.4	330.1	587.3	682.7	650.4
	# Eastern Region	64.4	143.4	287.9	491.6	560.0	521.8
	Central Region	30.6	78.7	164.3	269.8	324.1	315.8
	Western Region	27.6	85.8	193.9	301.6	367.4	344.0
Percentage (%)	**National**	**100.0**	**100.0**	**100.0**	**100.0**	**100.0**	**100.0**
	# Above County level	73.3	64.0	51.7	46.0	46.7	46.5
	County-level and below	26.7	36.0	48.3	54.0	53.3	53.5
	# Eastern Region	48.1	44.4	42.1	45.1	43.7	42.9
	Central Region	22.9	24.3	24.1	24.8	25.3	26.0
	Western Region	20.6	26.6	28.4	27.7	28.7	28.3

Notes:

[1] All the data of the communiqué are preliminary statistical data. Statistics of Hong Kong SAR, Macao SAR, and Taiwan are not included. Some of data are not compatible with the total of sub-entries due to rounding off.

[2] Cultural and tourism units refer to cultural institutions or business units that cultural and tourism administrations of all levels across the country organize or manage as related institutions in the cultural and tourism fields, excluding institutions organized or managed by authorities of press and publications, radio , film and television, etc. According to the current statistical system, the cultural institutions (such as public libraries, cultural centers, cultural stations, museums, state-owned art performance troupes and performing arts venues, etc.) organized by cultural authorities are all brought into the statistical range. Regarding business units managed as related institutions in the cultural and tourism fields, including private art performance troupes, for-profit venues, cybercafés, art dealers, show business agencies, Level-A tourist destinations, star hotels and travel agencies, related statistics are all included.

[3] The employees refer to the people who work with and receive payment from cultural and tourism administrations of all levels across the country organize or manage as related institutions in the cultural and tourism fields.

[4] The art performance troupes mean various professional artistic performance organizations organized by cultural institutions or to which the cultural and tourism administrations organize or manage as related institutions in the cultural and tourism fields (authorized by cultural and tourism authorities and with commercial performance license), and is engaged in such activities as performing arts, as well as professional private troupes (amateur part-time groups not included).

[5] An art museum refers to a state-owned art museum that cultural and tourism administrations organize or manage as related institutions in the cultural and tourism fields, with functions such as exhibitions, collections, research, public education, and other services, and is open to the public. It also refers to a non-profit private art museum that is registered with the civil affairs authorities and acknowledged by the cultural and tourism administrations with similar functions as above.

[6] Public libraries refer to libraries organized by cultural and tourism administrations for public use.

[7] The total number of books collected in public libraries refers to the sum of ancient books, books, collections of periodicals and newspapers, and manuals and manuscripts in the libraries'

catalogues, as well as audiovisual materials including micro-reproductions, videotapes, audio tapes and CDs.

[8] The total flow of person-time of public library refers to the gross visits made by the people to enjoy the services of the libraries in that year, including borrowing books, making inquiries and participating in readers' activities.

[9] The cultural institutions for mass public and communities refer to the places that cultural and tourism authorities at all levels organize for mass cultural activities, mainly including cultural centers (including comprehensive cultural centers and public art centers) and cultural stations.

[10] The number of activities refers to the sum of the activities including cultural, literary and artistic events, training classes, exhibitions, and public lectures.

[11] The cultural and arts groups refer to art groups composed by the staff members of the above-mentioned institutions that present non-profit art performances.

[12] A permanent exhibition refers to an exhibition in the museum at a fixed location which runs a long time.

[13] A temporary exhibition means an exhibition curated and installed by the museum, often varying in forms.

[14] Business units of cultural markets refer to the companies approved or acknowledged and have relevant licenses and filing documents, and that engage in cultural businesses and services. In line with the current statistical systems, the statistical range of business units of the cultural market includes for-profit show business venues, internet cafés, for-profit private art performance troupes, internet companies specialized in culture, art dealing companies and show business agencies.

[15] Cultural and tourism undertaking expense means aggregate of expenditures that the budget of all levels in the area invests to the cultural and tourism administrations. According to current statistical caliber, cultural operating expense does not include administrative expenditures of cultural and tourism administration and management departments at all levels.

[16] The Eastern region includes Beijing, Tianjin, Liaoning Province, Shanghai, Jiangsu Province, Fujian Province, Shandong Province, and Guangdong Province; Central region includes

Hebei Province, Shanxi Province, Jilin Province, Heilongjiang Province, Anhui Province, Jiangxi Province, Henan Province, Hubei Province, Hunan Province and Hainan Province; Western region includes Inner Mongolia (autonomous region), Guangxi (autonomous region), Chongqing, Sichuan Province, Guizhou Province, Yunan Province, Xizang (autonomous region), Shannxi Province, Gansu Province, Qinghai Province, Ningxia (autonomous region), and Xinjiang (autonomous region).